# Naked
## ON THE BUS

# Naked
## ON THE BUS

### ONE WOMAN'S JOURNEY TOLD
### THRU POETRY AND PROSE

SUZANNE MORGAN VARONA

"Your story is our priority"

LitPrime Solutions
21250 Hawthorne Blvd
Suite 500, Torrance, CA 90503
www.litprime.com
Phone: 1-800-981-9893

Published by LitPrime Solutions    10/28/2025

ISBN: 979-8-88703-136-1(sc)
ISBN: 979-8-88703-171-2(hc)
ISBN: 979-8-88703-137-8(e)

Library of Congress Control Number: 2022923982

# Contents

# Acknowledgements

A special thank you to my friends for their unswerving faith, support, and encouragement. They gave so much of their time and resources to make certain that my voice would be heard.

Thank you to all the great writers and philosophers who shared their wisdom and insights with the world and whose famous quotes I looked to for inspiration. Rick Moody, Oscar Wilde, Mark Twain, Maya Angelou, Princess Mara Ruspoli, Paul Williams, Josiah Royce, Plato, Don Henley, Glenn Frey, Anais Nin, Joseph Joubert, John Patrick Shanley.

# Perspective

So much of what I write is about pain, heartbreak and disillusionment. There are so many books that inspire us to feel good, pull ourselves up and out of our despair, and that's a good thing. But I also believe that we have to experience all the emotions we have, not bury them or hide from them. Shed those tears that want to be shed and feel the anger that builds up inside before it becomes a danger to us and to others. I think too much emphasis is put on feeling good all the time when it is only human to be sad when our heart is broken and angry when we are pushed to anger. Highs and lows, peaks and valleys, this is life. I have spent so much of my life feeling guilty that I wasn't tap dancing through it, that I finally decided to just feel what I feel when I feel it. I know there are millions of you out there who know exactly what I mean and so I say to you, "I love you, I know you and I understand you and you will see yourself in my words. There is no shame in that. It means you are human, you are not crazy and you are not alone. Take a ride on the bus with me."

# Foreword

What began as a reoccurring dream in my youth, later became the reality of my life. The dream of being on a bus and suddenly realizing that you have to get off at the next stop. You begin your walk down the aisle and become aware that all eyes are on you. What is it about you that is causing people to put down their newspapers, wake up from their naps, turn away from the windows and look in your direction? You glance down, trying to avoid the eyes of strangers and you see that you are naked. A wave of panic, disbelief and complete vulnerability takes over your body and knowing there is no place to hide, you stand, frozen in time. I always woke up then, shivering and sometimes, even crying. I remember feeling relieved that it had only been a dream, and yet, somehow the damage had been done. I still felt exposed and violated and afraid of ever letting anyone really see me. Naked on the bus, covered up in life. I became an enigma, even to myself.

# Free the Firefly

"Once when I was very small, and the
summer nights began to call, I chased a firefly
very far, and caught it in my special jar. As I
sat and pondered its destiny, I thought,
"What if that firefly were me?
And that is when I set it free."

Suzanne Morgan Varona

Freedom … I always craved it. I don't know when I changed from girl to woman, but it happened quickly. A woman trapped in a child's body. We've all been there, older than our years, somehow instinctively knowing things that no one ever taught us. I was confused by what I saw and what I heard around me. I remember threatening to run away, just for attention, a test of some kind, a manipulation played against the background of adolescence. I left a note behind and hid down the street in a neighbor's garage. The note said, "I'm running away. I hate you. Love, Suzy" For a very long time, I somehow confused the two emotions until I finally discovered that indifference was the difference.

# First Loves ... Mom and Dad

"When I was young and very small
I used to tiptoe down the hall
I'd fall asleep beside your door
I wasn't lonely anymore ...

As long as you were somewhere near
I never had a doubt or fear
And when I felt the need to cry
I knew that I could tell you why ...

I always felt so safe and sure
Whatever hurt, you had the cure
I knew that I was safe from harm
Inside the shelter of your arm ...

And now I've grown and gone away
I should have known I couldn't
stay I still reach out across the years
Needing you to still my fears ...

For nothing else can take the place
Of looking up to see your face
The one true love I'll ever know
Was in your eyes so long ago ..."

When you were divorced, after almost 30 years of marriage, something died in me. The rock I held tightly to crumbled and I never really felt safe again. Mom is dead now and Dad is so far away. I miss them beyond words and find that remembering them makes me wish that I had known them better and understood them more. Why does wisdom come to us so late, often too late to benefit from. Love is never enough … it just isn't, as much as we want it to be.

There were some lines from a film called "The Ice Storm" by Rick Moody that said:

"A family is like your own personal anti-matter. Your family is the void you emerge from and the place you return to when you die … and that's the paradox …

The closer you're drawn back in, the deeper into the void you go".

Has it ever been explained better that that?

# To Dad

You were so handsome, so mysterious, so charming, so wise. I learned to dance by standing on top of your feet as you twirled me around the room. I was intimidated by you, fascinated by you, afraid of you and comfortable with you. I spent hours listening to you speak, not wanting to miss one word, so sure that if I did, there would be a lesson missed that could change my life.

I saw myself in you, not physically, but internally, and I knew, from a very early age, that I carried your sensitivity, your despair, your humor and your quest for perfection. You care too much and so do I … you feel too deeply, and so do I … you never forget … and neither do I … you expect the best and deplore the worst in people … and so do I … above all, you value honesty and loyalty in your relationships … and so do I.

It wasn't easy being your daughter, but the things you taught me were the only things that gave me a compass to follow in my life … the lessons that I couldn't have survived without. Time and again, I would recall something you said, when I needed it the most, and it is because of you, that I am a decent person, albeit often a sad person, because when you expect perfection, you will always be disappointed. It was because I was yours, that I had the beautiful grandparents that I had and the blessed and charmed summers of my youth with them.

It is those days that have sustained me at the worst of times, those days that remind me that there is beauty and goodness in this world and that there are people who can love each other until the day they die and beyond.

I respect you and I love you. I know you because I am you and you are always with me, no matter how far apart we are.

You are my first love and my truest love.

# To Mom

"Although I wear the guise of child, bewitching in your sight, I, too, have my share of dreams and fancy taking flight … Yes, I am a little girl, but more than what I seem, an end to mommy's freedom, an extension of her dream …

Wishing that she wouldn't cry, I try to make her smile, wanting to believe that she'll be better in a while …

I will be her reason to go on and to survive, Taking joy from little things, so thankful she's alive …"

# The Beginning That Never Ended

(My puppy love, Roger)

He was a football hero with full lips and a curl that fell down over the middle of his forehead. He loved to sing "In the Still of the Night" with his buddies in a deep, baritone voice. He gave me the chills.

Remember when just holding hands could send shockwaves thru your body and how proud you felt when you entered a room with "Him."

He was the beginning of my womanhood, the stirring of my emotions, the devil that instilled feelings in me that I was never able to resolve. I discovered my core and I learned about passion and heartbreak and how to move on when love died. Puppy love can be the most devastating of all love because it is so raw, so new, and so unfamiliar. Once we survive the first heartbreak, then we know we can survive the ones to follow.

Even when it seems like we can't, we do.

# David ...
# High School Dreams

"Wrapped in his letter sweater ... my left hand hanging limp from the weight of his class ring, heavy with thread and nail polish to keep it from slipping off, we drove to the airport ... the old airport on the other side of Pittsburgh. Holding hands, we walked to one of the gates and watched the planes take off and land. I remember leaning against his chest, his arms around my waist, and together we dreamed of all the places we would go and all the things that we would do. Some feelings can never be recaptured in quite the same way as they felt the first time. I lived to dream again, many times, but never in quite the same innocent, magical way."

# Losing you

(David … my crush)

What is a dream but a wish
What is a wish but hope
What is hope but need
And where will all this lead?

I dream of a life with you
And I wish for my dream to come true
I hope that you need me too
But I know where all this will lead!

Around in a circle we go,
Continuing on the same path
Surely you see all the signs
In my eyes, in the way that I laugh.

There is nothing that I wouldn't do
To be closer, much closer to you
But I follow you round
In the circle I'm bound

And I'm losing, I'm losing … you.

# Letting the Good Ones Go

(The Perfect Walt)

You were a surprise
A gift
A sweet young man, with an open face and a gentle spirit
And you loved me.

You were kind to me, patient with me and I broke your heart.

I've always wanted to tell you how sorry I am and how often your face has haunted my dreams.

But it was so long ago and we are all grown up and if we passed on the street, we would probably not even recognize each other.

That's hard to believe because once I knew every curve of your face. the shape of your head and the sweetness of your lips, the way your sky-blue eyes squinted almost shut when you laughed or smiled.

You were special to me …
and I to you …
and I ruined it
and I'm so sorry.
I hope life has been good to you because you deserved it.

"Children begin by loving their parents; as they grow older they judge them; sometimes they forgive them."

Oscar Wilde

# And There You Were....
# (My Michelle)

I remember wishing long ago that I
might touch the sky
But I was told that heaven waits for
people when they die
I wouldn't let myself believe that heaven
wasn't here
And slowly I found bits of it in things
that I hold dear.

My sweet Michelle, I touched the sky, the day that I gave birth,
I found that heaven really is a place right here on earth.

# Angel Child

There's a special place inside me that I never knew was there
Until it came to life one day and I became aware
My world came into focus, the puzzle fell in place
And all I had to do was simply look into your face.

In your sweet face I found my joy, the sun came out to stay
And all the things that mattered once, got lost along the way
In all my life I never dreamed of loving as I do
A little girl with golden hair and searching eyes of blue.

I pray that I do right by you, but only time will tell,
If I deserved an angel child, my darling, my Michelle.

# Butterfly

You tiny little butterfly with bright and shining eyes
You dance through life with energy your fragileness belies
You make my life worth living, just by being who you are
You push my patience to the brink but never go too far
You know you have enslaved me, there is nothing I won't do
How strange to be imprisoned by a creature small as you
I watch you every second, seeing movement through my tears
Oh the dreams, the plans I have for you, the hopes and God, the fears.

As you pass so quickly through my life, I wish that time stood still
I want to keep you as you are, but I know I never will
To hold you fills an emptiness like water fills the sea
If I lost you, I'd lose everything, my life would cease to be
You are sunshine, you are rainbows, skin of pink and eyes of blue
You are laughter, you are roses, what is love? Michelle, it's you.

# Watching Her

She didn't know I was there; watching her as she approached the beautiful sleeping dog. A large dog, whose eyes, as they opened to view his admirer, were the color of his body, a soft brownish gray.

And my lovely child knelt down to him and their heads came together; her small, dear, shiny golden head against his, and with characteristic gentleness, she stroked him, and love filled the room.

My daughter, how much like me she is; to seek the quiet place amidst the noise, the gentle spirit among the strong; so much goodness in her, so much sweetness. Do others see her as I do? They must; for she radiates it, and often the light is blinding, as if looking upon the face of God.

I was filled with most incredible feeling of tenderness.

This then, is love.

# Suddenly

Suddenly, you're a woman
Suddenly, I don't know you anymore
Oh, there are some recognizable signs
But they are muted now
Colored by all the life experiences
That I wasn't a part of.

I thought I would always be aware
Of the changes you went through
The choices you made
The heartbreaks you suffered
I thought I would be the one you ran to
The way you did when you were a little girl.

I miss being needed by you
But I knew I had to raise you
With the courage to fly away
So fly away my little girl
And always know that I'm here
That I will always be here to hold you
And love you, to comfort you
When no one else will.

It's a mother thing … this unconditional thing,
It started when we stared into each other's eyes,
When you were a baby and I promised you everything
Always … and I meant it.

You are the me that I always wanted to be
Only better.
You are my daughter, my angel, my love
My reason.

So fly away little girl woman.
I'm here.

# Go

(Bill … Sorry is the only word)

I'm out in space, no end in sight
Holding air, in darkest night
I'm reaching out to feel your touch
A touch I love, and hate so much.

I'm torn in half, I can't decide
To run to you, or go and hide
I think that I have lost my mind
My eyes can see, but I am blind.

I wonder where the answers are
I'm tired of lies, I'm tired of war
There seems to be no peace for me
I'm in a trap, I must be free.

Hold me tight, but let me go
I'll break your heart, this much
I know I need to feel your love is true
But I am not the girl for you.

So go and live another life
A happy one, without your wife
But know that you will always be
No matter what, close to me.

# A Father's Good-by

(Silence speaks volumes) To Bill

He took us to dinner the night before we left, Michelle and her Mommy and Daddy, for the last time before the end.

The restaurant was dimly lit and there was a disco ball hanging from the ceiling in the middle of a small, empty dance floor.

The constant movement shot prisms of light throughout the room. Music was coming from somewhere and he asked her if she wanted to dance. She was so small and so lovely in her pretty dress. He led her to the dance floor and leaning over, he lifted her and placed her tiny feet on top of his and guided her around the floor.

As I watched with a strange mixture of finality and tenderness, the light caught them, her face looking up at him, his body bent over hers and one by one, his tears fell upon her golden head.

I felt as if a hand was wrapped tightly around my heart and for a moment I couldn't breathe.

I could feel my heart break and I knew it would never be whole again.

I will never forget that moment, it remains frozen in time
and it never stops hurting … and it never will.

21

"Are you so unobservant as not to have found out that sanity and happiness are an impossible combination?"

Mark Twain

# Who Am I?

"It's hard to view the world through eyes
that fill with misty tears
As close to death when young as when
we live a hundred years
As shiny as a diamond ring, as fleeting
as the wind
As dismal as a dying tree that slowly
starts to bend …

As fragile as a robin's wing, as tender as a sigh
As sudden as a summer rain, as empty as goodbye
As cheerful as a hummingbird, as soft as bunny hair
As stooped as fragile shoulders with a burden hard to bear …

As quiet as the ocean's depth, as distant as a star
Oh who is this I'm looking for; please tell me where you are
Can I find you in the shadows or in eyes I've never met?
Are you hiding in my secret thoughts in a place I've not found yet?

If I found you would I know you, would you have a face like mine?
Would your voice be low and gentle, would your hair be soft and fine?
You are all the things I speak of, things I am and want to be
That elusive cloud I reach for that is really … truly … me!"

Maya Angelou said, "A solitary fantasy can totally transform a million realities."

I never dealt with realities, only with my fantasies, and as a result, I find myself with nothing but my dreams … from being naked on a bus to sitting here at my computer trying to write something that might move someone to read my words and think, "Yes, I felt that way too. I had those same feelings and remember the same pain, frustration and wonder at the euphoric highs and devastating lows of life." I only know that I have to try and that is the miracle of fantasy. It helps you to believe that anything is possible.

# The Image

"Someone told me I was pretty … but I didn't see it.
Someone told me I was special … but I didn't feel it.
Someone, somewhere, told me a lot of things.
Why is believing so hard?

Are we what they say we are, or what we think we are?
In either case, we are only an image, different to everyone
who knows us.

I don't really care about anyone's opinion but my own. What scares
me is that I don't have an opinion. Is it because I don't know myself
well enough or because I'm afraid of the truth?"

"A place for my shelter, a person who's kind, why are the simple things hardest to find?"

Suzanne Morgan Varona

# Searching

"This search of mine is constant, with the longing glance of a shy admirer or the bold gaze of a dashing romancer; I look deep into the eyes of strangers and deeper into my own soul.

I listen for the words that will matter and brush tears from the eyes that have seen too much.

I study the fragile beauty of a wildflower and with infinite patience; I live with a society of hypocrites."

How sad to never taste the tears that come with each goodbye,
How sad to laugh your way through life, for you only live a lie.

Suzanne Morgan Varona

# The Far Side

I wonder what is waiting beyond the farthest hill,
Maybe there is emptiness that only love can fill.

How often in our daydreams do we see another place?
And long to leave this world behind and wear a different face.

We live inside a prison surrounded by our dreams.
Wearing sadness like a shroud, emitting silent screams.

We often talk of leaving, but never seem to go,
The sacrifice we're making, the joy we'll never know.

Before our time is past us, before our hearts are still,
We must find what is waiting on the far side of the hill.

There is a hurt inside me that will not go, it hangs there like a rock and strangles me. I cannot find the medicine to cure it, though my laughter sometimes eases the pain. Tenderness is like a balm, and love, well enough love, could kill the ache.

Suzanne Morgan Varona

"There is only one thing worse than being vulnerable
And that is not being vulnerable."

Princess Mara Ruspoli

# Take A Chance

Have you smiled at a face in the darkness?
Have you cried walking home in the rain?
Have you fallen in love for lifetime?
Just to find nothings left but the pain.

Have you ached with a longing for someone?
Have you reached for a hand in the night?
Have you breathed in the perfume of jasmine?
Have you stared at a seagull in flight?

Have you touched on the rim of tomorrow?
Have you squeezed every drop from today?
Have you found everyone to be different?
Living life in their own special way?

Have you given yourself to another?
Have you found what we're all searching for?
To be happy is just the beginning
To be loved is to have so much more.

If ever this life could be painless
If living was easy to do
Then nothing would have any meaning
Then nothing would ever be new.

We must go on smiling at strangers
We must throw our hats in the ring
Take a chance, take a dare, and go on living
For this life is a wonderful thing.

# Eyes

She looked into a thousand eyes that never saw her tears
Beyond the smiling lips, her eyes, betrayed the lonely years.

The reaching out and holding on and finally letting go,
Only eyes that truly see can ever really know.

So many secrets buried there, longing for release,
Her eyes will search a thousand more, for two that bring her peace.

# Cardboard Girl

Days go by, years go by, and still I cannot find
The only things I really want, true joy and peace of mind.

I fill my life with substitutes pretending they will do
But in the shadows of my mind, I know this isn't true.

The constant ache that grips my heart, is blotting out the sun
The only prize that matters is the prize I've never won.

Why can't I be the woman that I've always longed to be?
Someone special, someone different, there is only one of me.

What happened to that dreamy girl, with stardust in her eyes?
Who turned her back on truth and now has nothing but her lies.

When courage goes and fear remains, there is nowhere to go
And I became the cardboard girl that no one seems to know.

# Limbo

Something will always bring yesterday back to us,
But we can never go back again.

Haunting, bittersweet and painful are the memories
that hold me in limbo.

I cannot step backward, I cannot move forward
Is this then my destiny?
To remain afraid with half-closed eyes
afraid to look beyond this moment
and afraid not to.

"There are two kinds of people … those who listen, and those who wait to talk."

Paul Williams, Songwriter

# Lenny's Delusion

Many times I've reached for you
And found that you were gone
Often just a step away
And always moving on.

Slipping back into my life
Then slipping out again
One day soon to stay for good
But never saying when.

I have been a prisoner
While you have traveled free
Knowing deep within your heart
That always, you had me.

I never made you promises
And yet you always knew
You must have seen it in the eyes
That saw no one but you.

# Nemesis

God knows how I loved you
And only God knows why
We both have tried to kill it
But it doesn't want to die.

Love just doesn't go away
Like a headache or the rain
But lingers in a place that
Feeds on sadness and on pain.

Beyond our love we shared a dream
That never will come true
The promise of what might have been
Is locked in there with you.

You were a wild man, a gentle man, a little boy at play
I won't know you tomorrow, you are different everyday.
You dream the dreams of every man, but is there room for me?
I tried to share your life, but darling, that could never be.

# Analogy

(Lenny and Big Sur)

As I watched the surf rush up to meet the rocks,
Their brief but violent encounters recall to my mind our total
relationship.
Moments shared, not asked, but demanded,
A need so great it could not be refused.

Over and over again we came together, wanting
to speak the magic words, but finding instead
that our silence held all the answers.

We put distance between us only to find ourselves
closer, held by an invisible chain that neither of
us could break. At last, our time for reflection
revealed the truth about our relationship and
gave clarity to all that had gone before and all
that would follow.

I wandered into hell and it was … hell.

# Clarity

(That Moment)

She was only four years old. She said she was going to run away and I played along, believing it was only a game. I loved her so and she knew it. She was too little to leave her Mommy. She packed her tiny flowered bag, picked up her favorite stuffed animal and walked out the door on a chilly, gray, Colorado day.

I watched her silhouette grow smaller and smaller as she moved quickly down the street. I waited for her to turn around, to look back at me for comfort and assurance, but she didn't, she didn't look back … SHE DIDN'T LOOK BACK!!!

She turned the corner and disappeared from my sight. In that moment, I realized that my tiny little girl could walk away from me and never look back because looking back was more painful for her than facing the unknown and uncertainty of what lie ahead. She had seen too much and heard too much while living in the shadows of my fear of him.

I ran as if carried on the wings of angels and when I reached her, I swept her up in my arms and buried my head in her soft, warm neck. I quickly carried her in my arms back to the warmth of home without one word being spoken between us. We never talked about it again, but something changed inside me and inside her and my love for her gave me the courage to leave my prison and create a new beginning. For love of you, my darling Michelle, for love of you.

"Thinking is like loving and dying. Each of us must do it for himself."

Josiah Royce

# It's Now or Never...
# Jumping the fence...

Maybe it was just time...maybe it was those big blue 5 year old eyes that looked up at her and said "Do I have to come back here?" that jolted her into action. Whatever it was, she felt a surge of confidence that she could do this..that she had to do this...for those trusting blue eyes . Living in a volatile and abusive relationship had drained her of everything she once was until she became a stranger. Even to herself. Remembering the words of all women who observed the actions of abused women by saying "I would never put up with that... one slap and I would be out of there." "Ah yes. If only it were that easy. Fear freezes you into submission, mostly the fear that those you love will be hurt, because the abuser knows what your Achilles heel is, he knows how to play that card. Now she had some time to plan..knowing that those trusting blue eyes would be far away on a summer visit with her dad for two weeks...safely away. It was the night before that trip to Florida when she looked into those blue eyes and promised her that "No, honey, you don't have to come back here. The next time I see you, it will be just you and me in a brand new place, away from here". The promise was made and the promise would be kept.

Outwardly, this appeared to be a lovely young couple with a beautiful little girl and a cute black cocker spaniel named Smuggler. Out and about in Boulder, Colorado, charmed by this handsome and charismatic husband and father who drew people to him instantly. He didn't drink, he didn't do drugs, he was smart and athletic and ambitious. He had appeared in her life at a time when she was most vulnerable and the attraction was so intense that in retrospect she believed she had been bewitched in some way. Her mind stopped working and her body took over. He always played classical music and was an amazing dancer, 6'5 and slender, with the blackest hair and the bluest eyes, but dead eyes, like a shark...not the warm sweet appealing blue eyes of her little girl.

How she got here and what came before is another long s tory of its own, but suffice to say that the little girl was from a first marriage that failed, largely because of her own youth and inability to understand what love really was, especially the love of smart and successful older man who only wanted to make her happy. She felt smothered, lost and unsure of her feelings. Not understanding the gravity of her choices, she gave herself up to the moment, to whatever felt good at the time...not right, but good, not smart, but selfish, feeding her libido instead of her soul.

Memories are funny things. For her, the harder she tried to forget, the easier it was to remember. Dante said "One of our greatest sorrows is remembering when we were happy". Maybe it's that "compared to what" factor. She was always striving to see life through the eyes of the wonderful Japanese poet, Masahide who said "The barn burned down, now I can see the moon". Always conflicted, she found herself at a place in her life where survival became now or never and the stakes were high. There was the time that she awoke in the middle of the night, wild flowers scattered around her bruised face on the white pillow of their bed. She could make out his shadow, sitting in a chair in the corner, framed by the moonlight. When she stirred, he quickly came to her side, kneeling next to the bed, taking her hand and placing his head on her breast. "I'm so sorry, he said. I love you." She remembered feeling a numbness come over her, a deep despair in knowing that the reality wasn't that he didn't love her, that when you truly love someone, you don't beat them. It wasn't the first time and it wouldn't be the last. It didn't happen every day, not every week, but when it happened, it came out of nowhere, for no reason and that is the worst kind of abuse. You can't prepare for it, you can't stop it before it happens because the pattern is scattered, unpredictable. All you can do is walk the tightrope, every minute of every day, be as alert as you can to the signs. It could be frustration, exhaustion, a dead battery, a busy signal, a look on your face or in your eyes, but you didn't even know she was there. Always there was the knowledge that if you didn't find a way out, it pleased the life you treasured above all else in danger of being the target. As children do, this magical little creature with the bright blue eyes, sensed the tension. Sometimes when he came home and had his arms to her, she would run into his arms and he would swing her around in the air. Over his shoulder, her mother could see her sweet face, frozen in a smile knowing she was just being what she needed to be to keep the enemy at bay. Instinct, even in one so small, is a powerful thing. And so, when the time came and the little girl with the bright blue eyes was going away to a safe place for two weeks, she knew it was time to jump the fence and be on her way...away. He seldom left her alone, knowing deep inside that she would go, but his arrogance and ego wouldn't accept that reality. She took every free moment to plan her escape...to see a lawyer, obtain a restraining order and find a place to run to, a place where she would be safe and a place where her little blue eyed girl could come to her...away from here, just like she promised. Torn between needing help and not wanting to admit it, she chose her battles carefully. Knowing that everyone close to her could be at risk when she ran, she decided to contact a relative that she had seen at her grandfathers funeral a year before. He was a cousin of her fathers who came up to her during a gathering at her grandparents home and briefly took her aside. He told her that he had a sense that she was afraid of something...was she okay he asked. She felt her eyes fill with tears and she was unable to answer him. He gave her his card and told her that if she ever needed help, to call him, no questions asked and he would help her. His card was a business card, his business card, together with his name and phone number. He and his wife and their two little white poodles lived in Long Beach, California, where he had been in business for over 40 years. He had often been the discussion at the dinner table during the summer vacations of her youth, her grandmother referring to him as the black sheep of the family, the rebel son of her sister, who had run away to California as a young man and made his way to a successful life.

She said he was like a character from a Damon Runyon story and so he was. All she knew was that for now, he represented the light at the end of a very dark tunnel and she contacted him. She simply told him that she had to get away from an abusive situation and could he help her. His reply was simple. You're family, he said, I loved your grandfather. He always welcomed me and supported me when everyone else saw me as that character in California. I know how much he loved you and that's all I need to know. You have a place here as soon as you can get here. She then contacted a friend of her mother's who lived in Denver, asking if she could stay the night of her escape and take her to the airport the following day. Open arms prevailed and there were only two things left to do. Every Monday, the business they owned in Boulder was closed and together they drove to Denver to restock the business for the following week. She had to find a way to stay home that Monday, a way to find the time to move out while he was gone. The other thing was to contact a mover, give them a copy of the restraining order and then hold her breathe and pray. Those blue eyes had been gone a week now and it was the following Sunday before her move was planned. She could only hope that her attempt at pleading sickness the next day would convince him to let her stay home. In the midst of pretending, she actually became sick, running a temperature of 102, feeling dizzy and nauseous. He finally agreed that she should stay in bed and he left, just an hour before she had arranged for the movers to come. The tension that had built up inside her was paralyzing and she prayed for the strength to get thru this day without dying from the fear that consumed her. What if he returned early, what if he forgot something, what if his naturally suspicious nature brought him back before she was gone. She remembered the one other time that she tried to have him served with a restraining order and he changed the process service for blocks. She could never survive another aftermath to that scenario. The movers came and went quickly, as she didn't care about the furniture, didn't care about the material things, only about her daughters bedroom, her daughters toys and clothes and her own clothes. The important thing was to just get away, as quickly as she could. That night, she sat in the hallway of her mother's friends home, rocking back and forth in an old rocking chair and holding her stomach, crying and shaking and in disbelief that all this had happened to her, a child of intelligent, successful and loving parents, who had never been exposed to the unprovoked cruelty of one human being to another. And in the midst of her pain, she felt like a part of her was suddenly missing, a part that was destroying her, but a part that she had come to know as familiar somehow...kind of like a body part that became diseased and had to be removed before it affected the rest of her body. She had gotten used to it being there and now it was gone...a good thing, but leaving a hole where that diseased part had been. The next morning she flew off to begin a new life and await the return of the only thing that gave her the strength and motivation to begin again. To say that this chapter of her life was completely over, would be to say that when the Prince rode on his white horse over the hill with the fair maiden, the story ended there. There were many more chapters to be written and as with all things, endings are simply the beginnings of other new chapters. If there is anything to be learned by her story, it would be to say that if we have something that we love more than ourselves, then the tendency to be selfish, to just give in and give up, becomes impossible. Maybe for her the lesson to be learned was to try to love herself enough...but for her, that has always been the harder choice. Life goes on, and on, and on, but with the passage of time, some memories remain strong, lurking in the recesses of the mind, in the midnight hour.

# Moving on

No one else can do it
No one else but me
No longer can I run away
From all the things I see.

I always make excuses
For the things I say and do
I always sleep with strangers
And pretend that they are you.

Moving on beyond the dreams
That never will come true
Moving on beyond the need
I seem to have for you.

# The Eternal Optimist

(gleaned from a group encounter in Big Bear)

And so as I leave the sadness of all my yesterdays behind
And move anxiously toward the despair of all my tomorrows
I say this to you …

Take heart, for if the disappointment of today doesn't completely destroy you,
there is a pretty good chance that the one tomorrow will.
(Just kidding)????

# Forever is an 8 hour trip

(the Band Aids)

There is a look in the eyes that stare back from the mirror,
A knowing look
Disguised with innocence
And no small degree of hope.

A face and a body that sacrifices itself to a dream,
Over and over again
A dream that spans an eternity in 8 short hours
A 7 p.m. dream from which she awakens at 3 a.m.
The sound of the door as it closes behind him
The death knell of forever.

After the coy glances, the countless empty scotch glasses and
cigarette butts,
The too loud music and half-heard, half-felt conversation,
After the lies and the coming together
She knows, as she has always known
That forever is an 8-hour trip.

# After all

(Jack as my muse)

After the games are over
After the playing is done
Who will be crowned the winner?
What is the prize he won?

After the drinking and touching
After the sex and the lies
Nothing is left but the silence
After the laughter dies.

The world is full of people
With a wall around their hearts
To keep themselves from caring
Stop the hurt before it starts.

Although you were a stranger
I almost let you in
But I am a tired cynic
Whose dreams are wearing thin.

After we stop remembering
The hurt of another day
Then we will see each other
In a very different way.

Life is catching up with us
The time for games is past
And I am reaching out to find
A feeling that will last.

I'll always chase the rainbows
I'll always trip and fall
Without hoping, without wishing
There is nothing … after all.

# Just Friends?

(not with Jack)

There is a thing I can't define, partly yours and partly mine
Just a feeling, deep inside, a tenderness I try to hide

Somehow wanting you to know, I hate it when you have to go
Wondering if I should lie, caring, without knowing why

It isn't hard for me to see, that you would find more time for me
If there was caring in your heart, nothing would keep us apart

I don't need a sometime thing, wondering if the phone will ring
Now before the hurt is deep, I'll put the might-have-been to sleep

If I never feel your touch, then I won't miss it very much
Someone else will fill my mind, but friends are very hard to find

There will be another place, another girl without a face
Someone else who doesn't care, if sex is all you have to share

If you can't feel the same as I, if you don't even want to try
Then take the hand I offer now, let's just be friends, someway,
somehow.

# Dreams

Once I dreamed of golden sand
Once I held your strong, warm hand
Once I dreamed you'd always care
Now I'm holding only air.

Once I dreamed of fire light
Close to you on a snowy night
Once I dreamed of better days
Now we've gone our separate ways.

Once I dreamed of sharing life
To be your whore, your friend, your wife
Once I thought of only you
But dreams are dreams, they don't come true.

# Love, As a Woman Loves

It's funny how I never really listened before
To the sound of a door, a footstep, a voice.

To words.

I always thought I was a listener
And that I had heard it all.

I never knew how much more there was.

Looking back now
I can see that although we spent many hours talking to each other
We never really said anything.

I don't know who was more scared … you … or me.

# It's Simple

I can't help but wonder, if you really know
How lonely my world is when you have to go
People surround me in sight and in sound
But I stand alone, when you're not around.

Some things are simple, no need to explain
Your laughter brings sunshine
Your sorrow brings rain
Some things are simple, no need to explain.

# Denial

I need answers ... but I'm not sure of the questions
Maybe I don't really want to know.

Is this then, the real human tragedy?
To spend a lifetime seeking the answers
To questions that we run from
Frightened of the truth and the mirror it holds before us.

I wonder....

"I'm like the poet, dreamers we, who never write their song
I'm filled with good intentions, yes, but what did I do wrong?"

Suzanne Morgan Varona

Looking at you is like looking into a mirror
Different though we may look … we are the same.

It is frightening to know someone before you even speak.

# Reprieve

I search your face for answers, reading questions in your eyes,
We built hope on weak foundations, based on doubting, based on lies.

Love is nothing without sharing, all the good times and the bad,
Take my hand and walk beside me, I can't bear to see you sad.

Life goes by so very quickly, so much time is spent alone,
I embrace these special moments with the dearest love I've known.

And darling, when it's over and the magic fades away,
Someone else will bring the sunshine to a dark and dismal day.

# Soul mate

(Richard's profound presence)

When only Richard and Suzanne exist
And the world becomes part of our play
When you finally read in my silences
All that I'm trying to say

When you can believe in tomorrow
As much as you do in today
Then nothing can stop the reality
Nothing can stand in our way.

And now, as we share this journey together, please listen to me.
I want, I need, to feel you next to me to the very end. If the end
means over, then so be it. If the end means a new beginning, then
so be it. In this life, filled with uncertainty, I know only one thing
for certain …

I love you.

"All the sadness you're trying to avoid isn't worth all the happiness you're going to miss."

Plato

# Awakening

(Because of Salvatore)

How do I tell of the places I've been
and what has brought me to you?

How do I speak all the unspoken words
that have waited for your ears alone?

How does a cynic begin to believe again,
in all her lost dreams, and suddenly,
open the doors that were locked for so long?

Watching, I stand back from all this and hold
a part of myself in reserve, the part that is
always left to hold onto when all else is gone.

And yet, when you speak, I listen.

When you speak, I swallow your words like
a starving child and I live off of them for as
long as it takes.

# You and I

(Oh Salvatore ... Sal ... my dream)

You and I, we play at love, as thought it were a game
We try to keep things as they are, but nothing stays the same

We wish for happy hours, days of laughter, free of pain
Just two people sharing something, they might never find again

We won't think about tomorrow, just be happy for today
We will share these stolen hours then go softly on our way

Another time, another place, it could have been so sweet
But now it's touched by sadness, bitter feelings of defeat

If we part as better people, having loved and having lost
Then it's worth the price we have to pay, no matter what the cost

You and I, we're only human, we can't help the way we feel
Wanting someone to be close to is so honest and so real

If I touch your life with sunshine and you never ask me why
Then I'll go with fond remembrance, of two people, you and I.

There was something prophetic in this line from the film "Moonstruck"

"We are here to ruin ourselves
And to break our hearts
And love the wrong people
And die."

John Patrick Shanley

# Seasons

I loved you first in springtime, we burned the summer day
We married in the autumn and then winter came to stay

What happened to the sunshine, to the bright September leaves?
The sky is always cloudy now and my heart always grieves

A love to last forever, burning hot, a crimson blaze
Now it's over, I move slowly, walking blindly in a daze

Why is love a dying sunset, casting shadows on my life?
I was everything you wanted until I became your wife

All at once you didn't see me; I was nothing in your eyes
We drained everything from memories living only with our lies

So I leave you now in springtime, wanting only to be free
From the person you have made me, to the girl I want to be.

I have had some good times, I have shed some tears
I have walked in sunshine, I have lived with fears.

I have lain in solitude, and felt the empty place
Nothing left to cling to, just a pillow filling space.

Suzanne Morgan Varona

# A Losing War

Take the question out of why; take the rapture from a sigh
Take the petals from a rose and take my love before it grows

For as the sun can stop the rain, so can my laughter stop the pain
But if I love you more than now, I can't turn back, I won't know how

I feel with you a need to care, to find a life that we can share
But God how brief the time would be, before you needed more than me

We had our moment in the sun, we fought the battle and we won
But now it's time to close the door, the battle won, but not the war.

"When I look in the mirror a woman looks back
But under that frozen face
The soul of a child is lurking there
In a dark and secret place."

Suzanne Morgan Varona

# At Last

I look across a crowded room and search to find your face
I try to find a substitute for love I can't replace.

Our life together couldn't last; the hurt had gone too deep
Why can't I stop remembering and put the past to sleep?

I seem to walk the middle road; I don't know what to do
I'll never feel for anyone the way I felt for you.

If we could spend a lifetime making love and sharing dreams
Instead of killing every hope and yet, we can't, it seems.

I cannot keep you close to me when you are far away
Someone else with open arms will steal your heart someday.

If only I could let you go and never miss your touch
But that is asking for the moon, it's asking for too much.

So on we go, expecting time, to heal the painful past
Until one day we wake to find, that love is dead ... at last.

# Those Tender Years

Those tender years, oh how they flew
On wings as light as air
Those tender years when life was new
And living was a dare.

The special years, those tender years
When stars were diamond rings
And the sound of wind and crickets
Were the songs that an angel sings.

Those lovely years, the tender years
When rain meant God was sad
When puppies were our dearest friends
And snowfall made us glad.

How innocent, those tender years
When love was Mothers' touch
And all the cookies on the plate
Could never be too much.

How blissful were those tender years
When life was just a game
How sad to wake and find them gone
For nothing stays the same.

# *Reflections*

I stood upon the sandy bank
Of some forgotten stream
As I looked down, I saw my face
Reflected in a dream.

The wind caressed the leaves and grass
Then silence fell like rain
Two hands I felt but could not see
Wiped out my fear and pain.

My eyes looked up into the sky
The sun laughed in my face
The jumbled pieces of my life
Began to fall in place.

I've often thought about that day
That day so long ago
I've wondered who was there with me
And now at last I know.

I stood upon the threshold of
All past forgotten streams
And found my comfort from the ghost
Of a million broken dreams.

# Woman

A woman longs for simple things
Tied up in fancy bows
She wants to hear the pretty words
That no one seems to know.

She wants a man to lean on
Yet she needs to walk alone
She can't resist a baby's touch
A kiss, a ringing phone.

A woman feels another's pain
Her tears run fast and free
And she can see so many things
That no one else can see.

A woman takes a shattered dream
And makes it whole again
She doesn't long for yesterdays
And things that might have been.

And if you bring her candy corn
And daisies on a chain
She'll do without a diamond ring
And never cause you pain.

Just give her love and be there
When the days are dark and cold
Don't laugh at her when she is wrong
Or tell her she is old.

For beauty is a woman
She has earned it with her years
And in the eyes of those she loves
Its loss will bring her tears.

A woman is a fragile thing
But like the earth and seed
Her strength is found in knowing
She alone can fill our need.

# A Special Life

In this world of changing faces
Changing colors, changing minds
In this world beset with heartache
Take a moment to be kind.

There is pleasure all around you,
To be found in many ways
In the laughing eyes of children
In the brilliant autumn days.

As we suffer through a tragic war
And watch our heroes die
We must carry on regardless
Pick the pieces up and fly.

Treasure everything around you
Give till nothings left to give
Share yourself with those who need you
Find a special life to live.

"Desperado ... you better come to your senses
Get down from the fences and open the gate
You've got to let someone love you
before it's too late."

Don Henley and Glenn Fry

# Sharing the Dream

I felt the magic breath of spring
I touched a robin's fragile wing
My feet were wet with morning dew
And the world was a place
Where dreams come true.

I kissed a rose with tender lips
I tasted where the honey drips
I rested by a tiny brook
So lovely that it hurt to look.

I found a lovely willow tree
It wept with tears that fell on me
Its tired branches touched the ground
And the rustle of leaves was the only sound.

I held a puppy in my arms
A creature full of awkward charms
I felt its tongue against my face
A warmth the sun cannot replace.

I smiled at strangers everywhere
A smile is an easy gift to share
For what is living, too soon dies
And so I looked with hungry eyes.

All these moments came to be
While you were standing next to me
I found a world where dreams came true
Because I shared it all with you.

"This morning I wept.
I wept because the process by which I had become a woman was painful
And I wept
Because from now on I would weep less.

I wept
Because I had lost my pain
And I was not yet accustomed to its absence."

Anais Nin

# Just a Man and Mt. Suzanne

Things are different now
Life has taken on a different meaning
And when I look, suddenly, I see.

I feel enormous joy
Hampered by overwhelming dread
I look ahead with renewed optimism
Tempered by deadly caution.

In his eyes I can see forever
I can see myself
And I can see my fear.

I have conversations with myself
Late at night
My voice speaking words
My heart refuses to hear.

He is the beginning of all my possibilities
And the end to all my loneliness
He is the dragon slayer
The knight in shining Armor of all my dreams.

He is the person I trust the most
And distrust even more
I have given him what I refused to give
And nothing he can give me will ever be enough.

Sometimes I want to crawl back inside my skin
And pull down the shade
Back to the safe place where I lived for so long
Maybe that's where I belong

Maybe that solitary person
Is who I really am and need to be.

There is always a price to pay
Could it be that this time
The price is too high?
And if I don't pay it
Could the price be even higher?

He is, after all, just a man
And I
A mountain that is too high to climb.

# Survival

I threw a stone into the sea
I watched as down it fell
A timeless trip to paradise
A hurried trip to Hell.

Beneath the stillness and the calm
Beneath the tranquil blue
There waits a world beyond all worlds
That mortals ever knew.

A savage world of many forms,
Where only strength survives
The weak and gentle have no place
In which to live their lives.

For all who dare, for all who dream
For all with a beating heart
Learn to face a savage world
Right from the very start.

We fight our way into this world
The journey ahead is long
Survival is a primal thing
Meant only for the strong.

# The Answer Is ...

What makes life so hard to live?
What makes forgiving so hard to give?
What is this yearning for more, so much more?
Is living to die, never knowing the score?

Should life be a thing we just throw away?
Never saying the words we wish we could say
Never seeing the places we wish we could see
Never asking ourselves "What's the right path for me?"

What makes us special, what sets us apart?
What causes the fire that burns in our hearts?
What dreams do we cling to when all else is gone?
What brings on the daylight without any dawn?

What brings on the passion, the smiles and the tears?
What is missing somehow, through the days, through the years?
Where is the glimmer of light on a cold, rainy day?
The glimmer we leaned on to show us the way.

What makes us yearn to be strong, to be free?
What makes existence a turbulent sea?
What makes each ocean too far to cross?
What makes each winning end up as a loss?

Where are the answers we all need to know?
Why fight to keep what we finally let go?
I only know this and I learned it from living
None of it matters when you finally start giving.

"A part of kindness consists in loving people more than they deserve."

Joseph Joubert

# Slow Dance

A slow dance
Is the best dance
Taking time
While there is time
To know you
To learn your secret places
And find a way in.

It began quietly, slowly
As if waking from a dream
There was something

And soon, when I had a hurt
You felt it
When I had a thought
You voiced it
When there was a hunger
You fed it
No matter how great
No matter how deep.

Stay with me for now
There is only today to guide us
Past the doubt, into a place
Where there is no hurry
Just a long … slow … dance.

# The Gift

In remembering all the holidays that came before you
I remember that something was missing
It wasn't something I could taste, touch or see
Just a vague sense of space
Of empty places that I didn't know I had.

As I grew beyond the toys and games
I found that having things wasn't enough
And I wondered what was.

Watching, as your slow, easy smile lit up the room
I knew.

And now, as another holiday draws near
I want to tell you what your love has meant to me
What comfort I gain from the touch of your hand
And just the way you look at me
Is the only gift that really matters.

# Once

(Tony ... my prince ... my husband)

Once, we were magic.

Once we were lovers with endless
tomorrows
Finding the answers in each other's
eyes.

Once, there were words that were never good enough
And we longed to find a way to say what could never be said.

Once, I slept in the circle of your arms
Like a baby safe at its mother's breast
Nothing could hurt me then
I had my illusions
I had you.

How could I have known then
That the person I trusted the most
Would hurt me
Could hurt me
And take away everything that made me believe in love
In hope, in dreams, in magic.

How will I ever go back to being who I once was
Before you made me who I am?

# I Tried

(Oh Tony, how I tried)

Today I tried remembering
I tried to no avail
The quiet joy when you succeed
The anger when you fail.

I tried remembering who you were
Your face when you're asleep
A thousand little memories
I always meant to keep.

But you were then and this is now
And darling though I try
My mind keeps saying to my heart
He's gone ... let go ... good-by.

The sound of his key in the lock, my heart racing with anticipation to see his face and hear his voice ... knowing that I would rather be here than anywhere and that he would rather be anywhere but here. How do I explain the searing pain of knowing that it's over? This man who once adored me, now avoids my eyes, avoids my touch and I don't know why. I don't understand when he utters that worn out phrase "I love you Suzy, but I'm not in love with you". What does that mean?

# Ode to a Sad Ending

(au revoir Laureno)

Lying there, I'm hypnotized
I see the strangeness in your eyes
A funny look is on your face
And making love has left no trace.

Remembering the yesterdays,
Who told me someone always pays?
I gave you pain and now at last
You leave my body much too fast.

A shadow falls across your face
And something's gone I can't replace
You whistle the tune of a favorite song
But something is missing, something is wrong.

Everything dies, all the candles burn out
And love turns to sorrow, to pity and doubt
The pounding that I used to feel in my chest
Has slowed to a murmur, my heart is at rest.

Although you don't speak, I can still hear good-by
It's too late for questions, I won't ask you why
A physical love is a thing to behold
But the fire is brief and the ashes are cold.

# Missing You

Somewhere between the moon and the stars and the rising sun, I lose myself in thought.
There are times when I'm not sure if I will ever find my way back again …

Sleep won't come, but the memories will, and the pain is still with me … I cannot forget … maybe I don't want to forget … that you're gone … and I don't know why.

Would an answer have helped me forget sooner or would it have clouded my thoughts even more? Only the answer I wanted would count and you couldn't give me that.

"I love you darling, but I'm not in love with you" … what does that mean? What can that possibly mean? How many ways are there to love beyond just loving?

It is what it is and I can't face the morning sun without it … without the words from your lips, the look in your eyes and your hand touching mine as we pass in the hall.

The certainty of it all, the comfort of knowing there is love here when I come and when I go and now … as I face a new day … there is no certainty, no comfort lurking behind the curtains and under the covers or standing at the doorway.

You're gone and I'm empty and I cannot move from the place where you left me.

I can still smell you … you are everywhere.

I miss you.

# Without You

Without you what is there, to yearn for, to see
Without you what meaning does life have for me?

Without you the sunshine is hidden by rain
Without you my laughter is mingled with pain.

Without you the roses no longer smell sweet
Without you each goal meets with bitter defeat.

Without you the moonlight spreads magic no more
Without you I'm trapped in a room with no door.

Without you the world is a cruel, empty place
Without you I search, never finding your face.

Without you the stars lost their beauty somehow
Without you I'm nothing, what's left for me now?

Without you a kiss has no meaning at all
Without you my heart never answers its call.

Without you, I'm no one, for you made me real
Without you I touch, but I no longer feel.

Without you, I'm empty, I no longer care
Without you, existence is too much to bear.

Without you I live with my pain and my tears
Without you I know now, the worst of my fears.

# Love Stands Alone

It is said that there are many kinds of love, but for me, there is only one. It is an emotion that cries for expression, a feeling that cannot be denied, whether it be accepted, discarded, ignored, abused or returned. It always comes from the heart, not the head, and it always means something to the giver, if not always to the receiver.

There is love for a child, a parent, a sibling, a friend, a lover, an animal, humanity, a memory, a moment, a painting, a flower, all things, ad infinitum. Love hurts, but to live without loving is to never live at all. Beware those who fear love and fear being vulnerable to all it brings with it for in shutting out the bad, one also shuts out the good.

# Sanctuary

Maybe it was the easy laughter
The direct gaze
Or maybe just a heart that understood

Whatever it was, I knew, in an instant
That you would be the sister I never had
The teacher I wish I had
The friend I aspired to be

In you, I found a place to be who I really am
Even at my worst
A place where I am always forgiven
And a mirror to my better self

You gave me time when you had none to give
And sanctuary from the rain
And when the storm was over
You gave me reasons to smile again

A best friend is more than a companion
A best friend goes deeper
They are an audience to all your dreams
And down all the roads taken
They are always beside you

It can't be explained
It just is
And you just are.

# When It Rains In September

Where is the end of the beautiful rainbow?
Why do I love you and still let you go?
Wishing for storms and praying the rain
Will drown all my sorrow and wash away pain

Bring me a daisy with one golden eye
But turn away slowly and don't watch me cry
Give me your name but don't ask for my soul
I'm in so many halves that I'll never be whole

Touch me with tenderness, not with your hand
Or I'll slip thru your fingers like slim ropes of sand
Search out my face with a questioning stare
But don't let your lips touch the silk of my hair

Don't catch me watching the curve of your cheek
The words in my heart are the words I can't speak
When I look in the distance and find you're not there
I'll try not to notice, I'll try not to care

If I'm yours for the moment, then please make it brief
For time only adds to my unspoken grief
If I let myself love you and we become one
Then you'll fade like the colors too long in the sun

We said we would share in the here and the now
Anything more, I could never allow
Why do I cry without letting you know?
Why do I love you and still let you go?

Some men are forever, to trust and believe
But some touch the depths of your soul ... and then leave
Wave good-by but don't tell me, I won't ask you why
You are so like the wind that to live, you must fly

Treat me with tenderness only for now
And then when you leave, I'll manage somehow
I'll listen to lies and believe they are true
When it rains in September, I'll let go of you.

# The World of You and Me

The door was closed on all my dreams; my heart was safe from pain
I built a wall around myself, but I built the wall in vain

Never I said, will I fall in love, never will I give
But I saw your face and I felt your lips and I need those things to live

You are the reason I smile again, you are the reason I weep
You gave life to all the love that I had put to sleep

For suddenly this princess awoke and she began to feel
The face of my prince belonged to you and I knew that you were real

And yet there are moments when clouds appear and cover up the sun
Times when I ache to have you close, when I know I haven't won

I want to share your every dream and make them all come true
But love is just a fairy tale unless I'm holding you

So take my hand and take me to the place you want to be
There is nothing more important than the world of you and me.

Love for the ones I lost … Who left a hole in my heart

# Memories of Mom

The passage of time brings with it
Blurred memories
Faded photographs
And feelings so fragile
They almost break,
Disintegrating into a thousand pieces
And floating across the winter sky,
Searching for a place that can never be found again.

The place of my childhood,
The magic of Christmas
That only you could create.
The whispered words,
The smell of cookies and candles
Scraps of wrapping paper
And remnants of ribbons from a secret place.

You couldn't have known then
How much those moments sustained me
Through all the years that followed

When I put up my own tree
Baked my own cookies,
And wrapped my own presents
All the while yearning to be a child again,
Your child.

I want you to know Mom
That I haven't forgotten how hard you tried
To make everything special
And I want you to know that you succeeded.

I wish you a Christmas filled with the moments
And the memories
That you gave me.
I send with these words
The vision of a little girl
Making angels in the snow
And the mother who dried her mittens.

# To All The Brave Young Men

(For Andy, for them all)

With unkempt hair and timid eyes, your days are few and fast
The fun filled days had just begun, how sad they could not last
The hair of independence now lies shaved upon the floor
And your name becomes a number, you're not who you were before.
You're a soldier, you're a fighter, killing strangers in the dark,
Was it yesterday you laughed while playing football in the park?
Now the laughs are few, the game is real, each move is life or death
Each day becomes a treasure made more dear with every breath.
Not long ago, you dreamed a world of peace and love and joy
You become a man the hard way, with no time to be a boy
If the prayers of just one person, guides you safely thru the day
Then dear young man, heart of my heart, I'll pray, oh how I'll pray.
I'll stand by you in the dust and sand, I'll wipe away your tears,
I'll try to share the agony of all your hidden fears
I'll forgive you all the things you do, for I know you have no choice
Who will listen to the questions of a young and frightened voice?
Just come back to me, to all of us, for we long to touch your face
To find the words to thank you, dear young men of every race
I feel the loss of every life, I share the pain with you,
For with the death of brave young men, I die a little too.

# To Binkie

(my first dog) a little Scottish Terrier

You were simply a dog, small and black with sparkling eyes, yet to us you were happiness, you were special, you were pure. You never really knew hate or anger, you were loved and you knew it. You gave us all you could give and asked nothing in return. I learned about love from you, the unselfish kind, the unconditional kind.

You watched over us and kept us safe. You shared all our problems, even though you didn't understand them. Somehow you knew how to make everything better.

You had an uncanny knack for bringing the outside in and even now, now that you're gone, we still find your little collections of bones, leaves and socks … and it's like a dagger to the heart.

You are safe now, little girl, never again to feel pain, and that comforts us in our loneliness for you. There will be other dogs and other days to live without you, but there will never be another Binkie.

I miss you and love you and thank God you were in my life.

# Epilogue

Life is about choices, and for me, the bad choices were the greatest teachers. I learned from those choices and they led me to a place within myself where the pain and the lessons learned from the pain, became my poetry. There is a sensation of relief in the telling, a certain weightlessness that comes with throwing off the shackles of long held secrets and the truths that held me down. As with most of us, we are our own worst enemies as we stand in judgment of ourselves and our mistakes, seldom focusing on our successes. It is important to mourn the failures and the road not traveled and to wish and wonder at what might have been. It's all part of a life fully lived, each giving way to a true appreciation of how feeling bad teaches us how to appreciate feeling good, the yin and the yang. My thoughts go to moments, we all have them, those moments in time that stay with us through all our days.

Do I Speak of the euphoria I felt, running down a hospital corridor, my hospital gown thrown open in the back, my bare bottom visible to all, just to peer through the window at my first-born child?

Do I Speak of the depth of emotion that I felt each night as I fed her, looking deeply into her eyes and feeling the connection to another human being that is eternal and beyond description?

Do I Speak of her face as she showed me her engagement ring or the unbearable pain of watching her survive the end of her fairy tale?

Do I Speak of the phone call on a sunny California day when my parents told me they were going to divorce after almost 30 years of marriage? The only rock I had to cling to, crumbling into tiny pieces

Do I Speak of standing under a gazebo on a warm Saturday afternoon in Florida and saying I do for the first time to a man I was truly in love with? Or do I Speak of the constant hang up phone calls, followed by endless nights when he didn't come home?

Do I Speak of the countless Saturday nights with our best friends, listening to great music, cooking gourmet meals, appointing myself as the banker in our Monopoly games while stashing extra money, buying up all the properties, while the guys didn't have a clue. I miss the laughter, the camaraderie, the simple joy of those days.

Do I Speak of the phone calls from an ex-lover always on his way to a secret mission as an undercover agent? How he told me he would have a white carnation in his lapel when I met him for the first time at a crowded bar in Miami at happy hour. Do I Speak of how when I saw him across the room, the people and the noise disappeared completely and my feet left the ground? Yes, it really happened in just that way.

Do I Speak of Sundays in Long Beach when I took my little girl to the Marina to eat Artichokes with melted butter and how it made her feel so grown up and sophisticated to enjoy something so exotic.

Do I Speak of how surreal it was to move to a small town in Citrus County, Florida and to suddenly find our lives played out in the papers and on the radio, packing the tiny Courthouse at the City Council meetings every Thursday night?
Do I Speak about my soul mate, Richard, who could read my mind and think my thoughts and loved the little spot behind my right ear … who wrote me poetry, cried in my arms, went to my apartment when I wasn't there "just to sit in the chair where I had sat", but couldn't make love to me?

Do I Speak about the rainy day in Boston, in the back of a cab, on the way to his 20-year reunion at Harvard, when I noticed the ketchup on his tie, his one brown sock and one black sock, and how the love I felt for him at that moment took my breath away?

Do I Speak of seeing my beloved grandfather at his funeral and coming face to face, for the first time, with the realization that good things don't always last forever. It's over 30 years now and my heart still aches for him.

Do I try to explain how for me, the greatest love story of all time is the one between Alfredo and Salvatore in Cinema Paradiso? I have never seen such pure, unselfish and unconditional love as that between an aging projectionist, long past his youthful dreams, and the young boy who needed a father. The music, the beauty, the magic of that film is always with me because for me, that is what love should be.

Do I Speak of how I finally understood my mother and all that she was and all that she did, after she died. How much I miss her ... so caught up in wanting her while she was alive that I never realized that she was really there for me all the time. Oh Mom, I finally know you and now I can't tell you so.

So many things to speak of, special only to me, common to most of us and yet blinding colors on the canvas that became my life.

It seems as though there was always a sadness inside me. I couldn't put a word to it when I was small. I just wanted and needed to believe that all was right in my world. It's funny how children can create a world of their own in order to make living there okay.

And now, as I find myself approaching the final years of my life, I am doing what I have always dreamed of doing. I am doing what I was meant to do and never did. Those dreams of being naked on the bus stayed with me and closed me off from putting myself out there to be judged. But one day we wake up and realize that there aren't going to be many more days left to follow that one dream that won't go away ... the dream more powerful than being naked on the bus … the dream that my words might touch someone, somehow, in some way that matters. "Hey, I felt just like that once" or "I'm going through the same thing now". I'm here to tell you that it's okay and you will be too. Trust me. I've been there. I'm there now. It's called "Life".